Michelle Obama

Tadashi Shoji

PLATE 1

PLATE 2

Carolina Herrera

Kenzo

PLATE 3

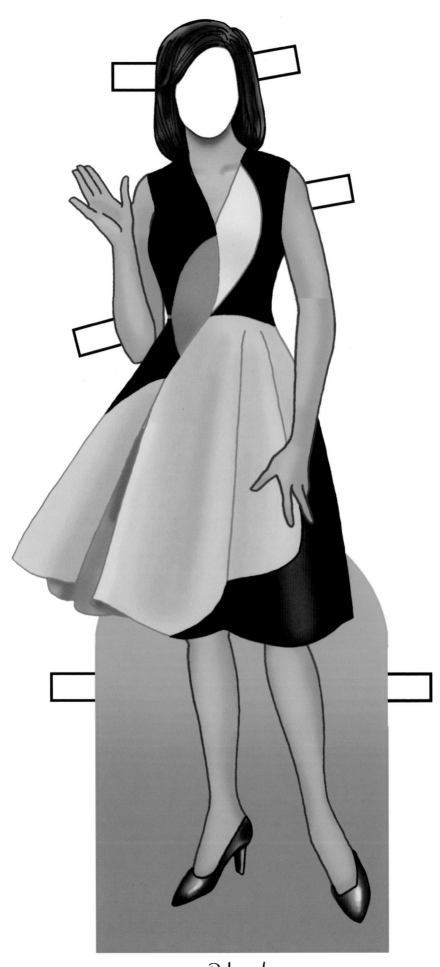

PLATE 4

Roksanda

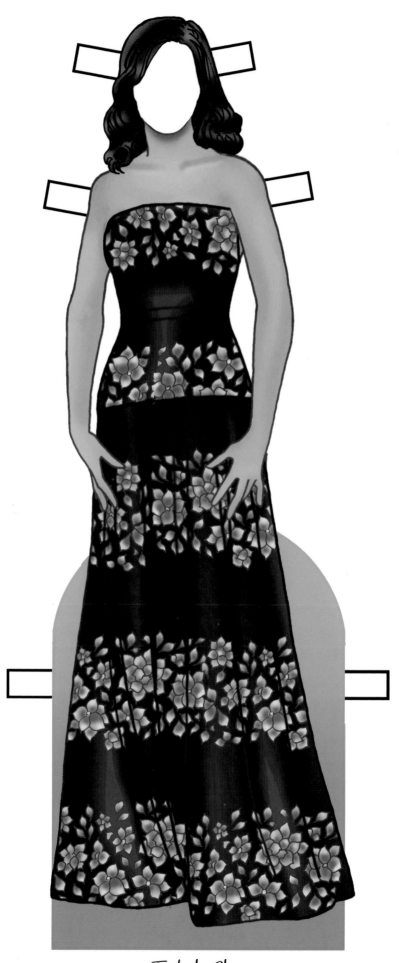

Tadashi Shoji

PLATE 5

PLATE 6

Vera Wang

Oscar de la Renta

PLATE 7

Naeem Khan

PLATE 8

Narciso Rodriguez

PLATE 9

PLATE 10

Naeem Khan

Gucci

PLATE 11

Naeem Khan

PLATE 12

Tracy Reese

PLATE 13

PLATE 14

Jason Wu

Brandon Maxwell

PLATE 15

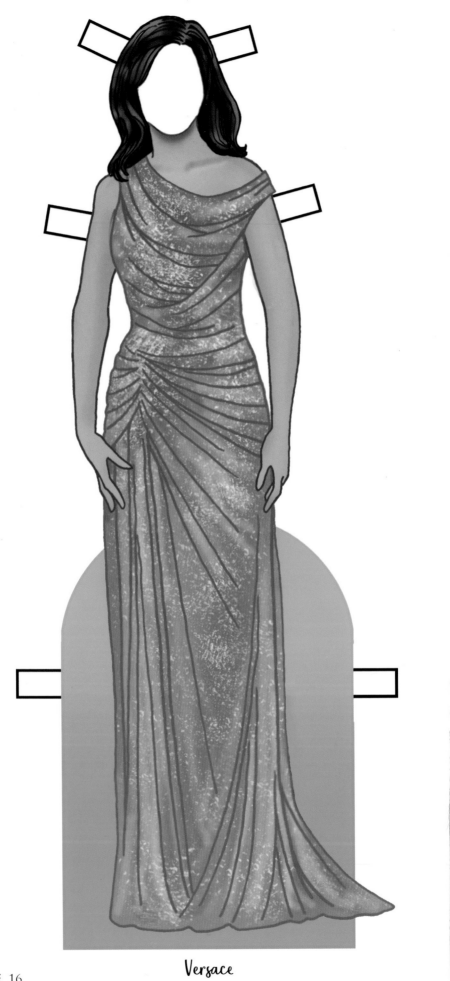

Versace

PLATE 16